How Things Move

Changing Direction

Siân Smith

Raintree

www.raintreepublishers.co.uk
Visit our website to find out more information about Raintree books.

To order:

☎ Phone 0845 6044371

▤ Fax +44 (0) 1865 312263

▥ Email myorders@capstonepub.co.uk

Customers from outside the UK please telephone +44 1865 312262

Raintree is an imprint of Capstone Global Library Limited, a company incorporated in England and Wales having its registered office at 7 Pilgrim Street, London, EC4V 6LB – Registered company number: 6695582

Edited by Sian Smith, Rebecca Rissman, and Charlotte Guillain
Designed by Joanna Hinton-Malivoire
Picture research by Elizabeth Alexander
Production by Duncan Gilbert
Originated by Dot Gradations Ltd
Printed and bound in China by South China Printing Company Ltd

ISBN 978 0 431 19324 3 (hardback)
13 12 11 10 09
10 9 8 7 6 5 4 3 2 1

ISBN 978 0 431 19330 4 (paperback)
14 13 12 11 10
10 9 8 7 6 5 4 3 2 1

British Library Cataloguing in Publication Data
Smith, Sian
    Changing direction. - (How things move)
    1. Translational motion - Juvenile literature
    I. Title
    531.1'13

Acknowledgements
We would would like to thank the following for permission to reproduce photographs: ©Capstone Global Library Ltd. p.**14** (Tudor Photography 2004); ©Corbis pp.**15** (Ajax/zefa), **21** (Joson/zefa), **16** (Roy Dabner/epa); ©Getty Images pp.**17**, **23 bottom** (Julian Finney/Staff, Getty Images Sport), **7** (Panoramic Images), **6**, **23 top** (Stone/Greg Pease), **11** (The Image Bank/Paul Taylor); ©iStockphoto.com pp.**19** (Kris Hanke), **20** (Oktay Ortakcioglu); ©Photolibrary pp.**8** (Brand X Pictures/Steve Allen) **9** (image100), **18**, **23 middle** (It Stock RM), **5** (Tom Bonaventure/ Photographer's Choice); © Punchstock p.**10** (Digital Vision); ©Shutterstock pp.**12** (Vladimir Ivanovich Danilov), **4** (@erics), **13** (Four Oaks)

Cover photograph of a surfer reproduced with permission of ©Getty Images (2006 Jason Childs). Back cover photograph of a kite reproduced with permission of ©iStockphoto.com (Kris Hanke).

Every effort has been made to contact copyright holders of material reproduced in this book. Any omissions will be rectified in subsequent printings if notice is given to the publishers.

Contents

Moving

Things can move in many ways.

Things can move fast or slowly.

Direction

The way something is going is called its direction.

Things can move in many directions.

Things can move up.

Things can move down.

Things can move forwards.

Things can move backwards.

Changing direction

Things can change direction.

When something changes direction it moves towards a different place.

This see-saw changes direction.
It moves up and down.

This swing changes direction.
It moves backwards and forwards.

Pushes and pulls

Pushing something can change its direction.

A push can change the direction
of a ball.

Pulling something can change
its direction.

A pull can change the direction
of a kite.

Different directions

Things can move in many different directions.

Can you change direction?

What have you learned?

- The way something is going is called its direction.

- A push can make something change direction.

- A pull can make something change direction.

Picture glossary

direction way something is going

pull make something move towards you

push make something move away from you

Index

Notes for parents and teachers
Before reading
Talk to the children about direction. Demonstrate moving in different directions for example, by taking one step forwards, two steps back, turning around, moving diagonally.

After reading
• In the hall give children some instructions on how to move in different directions. For example, take two big steps forward. Take one step to the left. Take five small steps backwards. Take two steps to the right. Turn around. Sit down.
• Draw a simple maze on a board. Ask children to give you instructions to get to the centre.